IMPERFRACTIONS

Fragments of becoming

Haasa

BookLeaf Publishing
India | USA | UK

Made with ❤ on the BookLeaf Publishing Platform
www.bookleafpub.in
www.bookleafpub.com

Dedication

To my family, for shaping me into who I am. To my friends, for their presence and absence alike. To the acquaintances who sparked my growth and the brief guiders who taught me what matters. And to myself, for finding strength in moments of doubt. Each of you has guided me on this journey.

Preface

This book reflects my journey—moments of growth, self-discovery, and the lessons learned along the way. Each poem represents a chapter of my experiences, and through these words, I hope to connect with those who have felt similar emotions. Writing has been a powerful tool for self-expression and healing, and it is with that same intention that I share this work. May these poems resonate with you and offer a glimpse into the shared experiences that unite us all.

Acknowledgements

I would like to express my heartfelt gratitude to everyone who has been a part of this journey. To my mom, whose unwavering mental support has been a constant source of strength, and to my brothers, for their encouragement and understanding during this process.

A special thanks to Rajashekar and Sreeja, whose insightful feedback helped shape these poems into what they are today, and to Likhitha, for guiding me when I needed direction. I am also deeply grateful to my readers, whose belief in my work motivates me to keep creating.

1.Flare

A POET'S MIND

The powerful silence as we read,
In a kingdom of words that we lead,
Out of context, it may seem—
It's all in the mind and the dream.
Beneath the oceans and beyond the sky,
A poet's soul wanders by;
A lost cause, one might say,
Where fleeting comments fade away.
Yet still, we find a way
To put down the words as we may.

In the quiet corners of the night,
Ink and thought take daring flight;
Every whisper of emotion untold
Finds shelter in verses bold.
The pen becomes a sacred sword,
Carving tales from deep accord,
Each line a timeless, gentle trace
In the boundless realms of grace.

SOULSHINE

I woke up today, waiting for the sun,
Looking for him, 'cause talking to him is fun.
He peeped through the clouds and shyed away,
Longing to come out like a kid who wants to play.

He mustered up the courage for the folks,
To share some stories and crack a few jokes.
And when he rose, he lit the sky,
The wind blew and the birds flew high.

Looking at him, I shared a smile,
Chatted with him for a while.
He looked down and said to me,
"How does it feel to be set free?"

I realized that he'd go down soon,
So I kissed goodbye and welcomed the moon.

THAT KIND OF LOVE

That kind of love in ancient scripts is what I yearn for—
It reads, "For a lifetime, my heart belongs only to her."
That kind of love is rare to find,
So cruel to the heart, for it captures the mind.
That kind of love is caring for each other,
With the gentleness and warmth of a mother.
That kind of love is hidden within our bodies,
Two souls colliding, escaping the world's tragedies.
That kind of love is like opposite poles,
Drawn to each other, entwining their souls.

ENCHANTED

To fall in love with him, I had my reasons,
But my love won't change, not even with seasons.
No, I didn't fall in love at first sight,
Yet he held onto hope, believing I might.

And I did fall in love—I keep falling every time he
crosses my mind, but don't ask me how.
Why I fell for him is still tragic,
But what happened between us? Pure magic.

Searching for answers in those ocean-deep eyes,
What's in his smile is the answer, I realize.
I realize—it's an excuse I just use,
But I fell for all of him, and he's the one I'll always
choose.

He stole all my pieces by chance,
I'm content to be held by his glance.
I will love him even as we grow shorter to the ground,
And deep within the earth, our love will still be found.

MY MUSE

He is like the poetry in my notes,
And the sweet, adorable quotes.
This man makes me scribble for hours,
Just to write him a letter saying, "I'm yours."

For his deep brown eyes,
I melt like ice.
And he has no clue
That he is my dream come true.

2.Flicker

REGRETS

What if we hadn't kissed that night?
I wouldn't have held on to hope,
Or searched for ways to help me cope.
I wouldn't have cried every night,
Longing for reassurance after our fight.
I wouldn't call your name again,
Just to watch our ending begin.
Instead, I would have turned memories around,
Deluded—smiling, as if we were perfectly found.

WHEN STARS FALL

I wished on every fragment of star for you,
But even the shattered light couldn't bring you through
I don't blame the stars that died–
I blame myself
for wishing on something dead
for someone alive.

DAD'S FADING FACE

I realize his memories are slowly fading away;
I can no longer clearly recall his face.
Right now, I wish he were to stay—
Stay longer, giving me moments to embrace.

I never thought he would leave,
Gone so far, beyond my reach and voice.
His absence is the ache I grieve;
If I had known, I would have held him tight—
never letting go—when I still had the choice.

HALF-READ LETTERS

Out of all the letters I wrote to him in my head,
I found a memory covered in red.
I held my head in my hands,
To not let my heart slip away by chance.
Not daring to open the past,
I stitched it shut, hoping it would last.

But I guess I pulled too hard, for the memory broke,
Flowing into my eyes as they spoke.
Turning away from hope, I ran into despair,
Gasping for a heavy chunk of air.
Telling myself that I'll forget him,
Yet for his voice, I'm still a victim.
How could I ever let him go?
I can't—and that's all I know.
To love him with all my mind,
With all the consciousness that I may find.

As the door creaks, I turn my head,
My mama tells me to go to bed.
Hit by reality, I watched the clock strike one,
Washing away our memories of fun.
After all, time lets everything pass by...
So what is it, then? Was everything a lie?

POV: I THINK HE KNOWS TOO

I visit him every day with flowers in my hand,
Reading him stories, tuning to our favourite band.
And when he asks me about love,
How can I explain it to him now?
That you're the one who occupies my mind,
And that I search for your presence in every place I find.
For him, wouldn't it be too harsh?
His heart—I know it will definitely crash.

I catch him reading, deep into my actions,
I knew he'd figure it out soon, given the abstractions.
But he'd never ask me a question,
And I'd never make any confession.

BATTLES LOST

Belittling her emotions, she was kept quiet.
A small conversation would turn into a big fight.
Daylight scared her—too harsh, too bright.
Her voice echoed in the ears of owls in the night,
Yearning for trust, a safe place, and white.
She was twisted, but could just stand right,
Balancing everything despite the plight.

LIKE MY MOTHER

I see her, I see myself in her eyes.
I see myself turning into a mini version of her.
I see the price I have to pay for being too nice.
I see everything around me, soft and blur.

What can I do to help?
What can I do to get out of the cycle that won't stop?
What can I offer to myself–
A chance to rise instead of drop?

HEY, LIL MISS

She looked at me, carrying hope in her eyes,
A smile so bright and a personality so nice.
I looked away as I saw her innocent face,
How could I tell her we're not in the same phase?

It would break her heart,
If I told her that the world tore her apart.
So I was forced to keep quiet,
And look back at her, hiding my plight.

3.Furnace

INK AND ECHOES

She leaves words on her pages, fragments reflecting her
immense brokenness.
She yearns for a break from this feeling, yet finds herself
staring at the ceiling,
Wondering what caused the void in her—
And maybe, just maybe, she could disappear.

But her voices ring a bell in her mind,
A gentle reminder she can still find.
So, she writes—hoping the words will mend,
Or at least hold her together until the end.

LET GO

Just watching airplanes leave
Feels like hearts learning to grieve.
It reminds me of letting dear ones go—
Not with anger, just a silent flow.

They said they'd come back—I used to believe,
Till I heard, "Let bygones be bygones," and chose to breathe.
But how do we say goodbye with no end?
No final word, no time to mend?

A part of me still holds that door,
Where memories linger, soft and sore.
And though I try to walk away,
I stumble on the things they didn't say.

Letting go isn't always loud—
Sometimes, it's just watching clouds,
Hoping they'll carry the weight of what we'll never know,
As we learn, slowly, to let them go.

BUT WHY DO WE GO BACK?

I always wondered why people
watch the same movie again and again.
When I asked my friends,
they said—"It's for the plot."
My mom said—"It is to bring back the time."
Few said—"It's to relive the moments."

But one voice stayed with me—
quiet, honest, different.
It said,
"It feels new every time I watch it.
Because I change,
and the movie shows me that."

And maybe that's true.
Maybe we don't watch it for the film.
Maybe we watch it
to see how far we've come.

BELIEF

I sat there, sat in silence
A gentle voice reciting the stories in my head,
Reading thoroughly and telling me my resilience—
That I can make it through as I lead.

Belief is underused, definitely,
For I could tell that the voice in my mind definitely did,
Did believe in me—astonishingly, unconditionally,
Believed in the abilities that I myself hid.

I listened to it with all my ability,
Taking the path—to the places it took me to.
It showed me my strength—my agility,
Something I discovered, something new.

It was unfamiliar, mysterious in a way,
Yet in me, it attracted all the stars from within.
I knew my stars—what they represented and what they say,
They whispered of triumphs that lit up my day and made my soul grin.

WARM GAZE

In the form of rain, you relieve my pain,
Falling on my cheeks, I feel I've reached the peaks.

There you come with the breeze,
Shaking the branches of the trees.
It feels like you pat my head,
Bringing comfort, like when I'm in bed.

You are a connection to every heart,
Helping each one realize their part.
Healing souls that faced hardship,
You offer them your endless friendship.

Healing those who've faced despair,
With gentle presence, always there.
We search for you with longing eyes,
But can't find you in a world full of lies.

Like a sparkle, you shine so bright—
It's always the heart that sees what's right.

ARMS AROUND

Sometimes words don't know what to say,
But arms do—when they wrap and stay.
A hug doesn't ask, it doesn't pry,
It simply holds you when you cry.

In that moment, the world starts to slow,
Pain fades gently, like melting snow.
Laughter feels lighter when shared skin to skin,
And battles feel smaller, hugged from within.

Whether from a friend or someone new,
A hug says "I see the soul in you."
It's warmth, it's safety, it's home in disguise—
A quiet place where healing lies.

MOMO

They say many soul encounters aren't permanent,
However, I could clearly tell that ours is different.
You are the phase of my life that never fades,
A chapter I carry to every page.
As crazy as it might sound,
You magically appear whenever I need you around.
Friendship so silly and deep,
Our story is a real keep.
In a world full of empty promises,
Let me be your warm embrace.
If there's one thing I'd wish the stars,
I'd wish our friendship to everlast.

BETWEEN FIGHTS AND LAUGHTER

I call your name to order you around,
But when I repeat it, I still don't hear a sound.
Looking around the empty space,
I shrugged and smiled, recalling your voice and face.
For some reason, I missed you a lot,
As all the memories in my mind got caught.
I missed you more when I saw my empty cup—
Remembering how we'd argue when you'd refuse to fill it up.
I stole your snacks just to watch you furious
Your angry rants—always so serious.

I miss your laugh, your silly little fight,
The way we'd joke from morning to night.
And how you'd side-glare when I flexed my hair,
As if to say, "You're not even close to fair."
And damn, I wish I could relive the stupid bond we share.

Now every little thing reminds me of you—
The socks on the floor, that one broken shoe.
And though we bickered more than we agreed,
You're the piece of my heart I'll always need.
Now this silence echoes, and I can't pretend,
I wish you were here, my brother, my friend.

HIS MUSE

He looked like a poet, I could tell.
His eyes met mine – I'd never felt more defined,
As a beauty that, through his gaze, chimed.
He smiled at me, waving his hand,
The rush of blood to my cheeks was definitely not
something I had planned.
He made me feel like I'm the art
He's been painting, pouring out his heart.
He read through me like an open book,
Each word–each breath–was all it took.
I caught him staring at me endlessly,
As if I were a song, sung silently.
In his eyes, I found a world so surreal,
A place where only my soul could heal.
He's the one who knew my depths too well to quell.

BATTLES WON

She broke the chains that held her tight.
Now walks with ease in morning light.
She leans on love, her truest right,
Their hands held hers through every fright.
With every step, she feels more bright—
And claims the day once ruled by night.